Drawing Fairies, Mermaids, and Unicorns

Jorge Santillan and Sarah Eason

Gareth Stevens
Publishing

Please visit our website, www.garethstevens.com. For a free color catalog of all our high-quality books, call toll free 1-800-542-2595 or fax 1-877-542-2596.

Library of Congress Cataloging-in-Publication Data

Eason, Sarah.
 Drawing fairies, mermaids, and unicorns / Sarah Eason.
    pages cm. — (Learn to draw)
ISBN 978-1-4339-9537-8 (pbk.)
ISBN 978-1-4339-9538-5
ISBN 978-1-4339-9536-1 (library binding)
1. Fairies in art—Juvenile literature. 2. Animals, Mythical, in art—Juvenile literature. 3. Drawing—Technique—Juvenile literature. I. Title.
 NC825.F22E27 2013
 743'.87—dc23
                                       2012048243

Published in 2014 by
Gareth Stevens Publishing
111 East 14th Street, Suite 349
New York, NY 10003

© 2014 Gareth Stevens Publishing

Produced for Gareth Stevens by Calcium Creative Ltd
Illustrated by Jorge Santillan
Designed by Paul Myerscough
Edited by Rachel Blount

All rights reserved. No part of this book may be reproduced in any form without permission from the publisher, except by reviewer.

Printed in the United States of America

CPSIA compliance information: Batch CS13GS: For further information contact Gareth Stevens, New York, New York at 1-800-542-2595.

Contents

Learn to Draw! 4
Forest Fairies 6
Water Fairies 10
Fire Fairies 14
Beautiful Mermaids 18
Powerful Unicorns 22
Flying Unicorns 26
Glossary 30
For More Information 31
Index 32

Learn to Draw!

Fairies, mermaids, and unicorns are truly magical creatures. They can be found in many wonderful stories and pictures, and some people even say they have seen these beautiful beings in real life. We'll show you how to draw fairies, mermaids, and unicorns—and if you really believe in them, perhaps you might see one in real life, too!

You will need:

Just a few simple pieces of equipment are needed to create beautiful drawings of fairies, mermaids, and unicorns:

Sketchpad or paper
Visit an art store to buy good quality paper.

Pencils
You will need both fine-tipped and thick-tipped pencils.

Eraser
Don't worry if you make a mistake—use an eraser to remove any unwanted lines. You can even use it to add highlights.

Paintbrush, paints, and pens
Buy a set of quality paints, brushes, and coloring pens to add color to your pretty drawings.

Forest Fairies

Have you ever heard a rustle in the woods? It may have been a bird or a bear—or perhaps a forest fairy hiding out of sight! The forest is full of pretty fairies that flit from tree to tree. So next time you take a walk in the woods, look out for fairy friends!

Step 1

Draw the fairy's body and dress. Then draw her head, arms, hands, wand, legs, and feet. Draw crescents for the fairy's wings.

Step 2

Now add the fairy's hair, ears, and eyes. Draw the leaf collar and the fairy's dress. Erase the rough lines from step 1.

Step 3

Add detail to the eyes, and draw the nose and mouth. Pencil the fingers, boots, leaf bracelet, and the magic twig wand. Add the antennae.

Step 4

Pencil the folds on the fairy's dress and the lines on her wings.

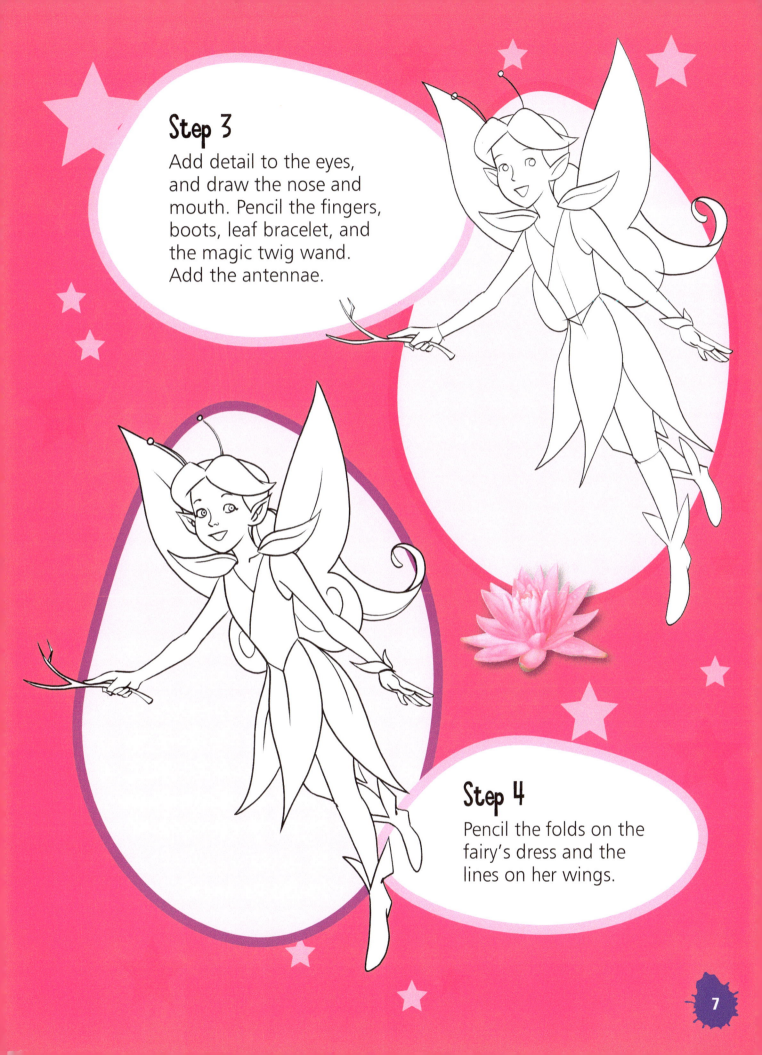

Step 5

Add shading to the fairy's dress, wings, hair, and face. Don't forget to shade her arms, hands, legs, and boots, too.

Step 6

Now you can start to color your fairy. Use a dark green for the fairy's skirt, boots, leaf bracelet, and leaf collar. Paint the bodice of her dress light green. Color the wings light blue and give your fairy rich red-brown hair. This fairy has bright green eyes to match her dress!

Step 7

Bring your fairy to life with touches of white for highlights. Add highlights to the wings, hair, face, arms, legs, and dress. Your cute forest fairy is now complete!

Forest Hiding Holes

Foxglove flowers grow wild in many forest places. Little forest fairies love the foxglove because it is a perfect hiding place! The pretty fairies sit inside the "cup" of the flower—and peek out at passersby. Some people say that the foxglove flower even bends down from its stalk to say "hello" to nearby fairies!

Water Fairies

Fairies that live in water are tiny creatures that are rarely seen. People have believed in water fairies for thousands of years. Some say they have seen fairies flitting through the water like tiny darts of light. Others claim they have seen beautiful fairies, like this pretty water fairy, flying above rivers and streams.

Step 1

Draw the fairy's body and dress. Then draw her head, arms, hands, legs, and feet. Add her wings.

Step 2

Go over the lines from step 1 to draw the outline of the fairy. Erase the rough lines you drew in step 1. Pencil the fairy's eyes, ear, and hands.

Step 3

Now begin to add detail. Draw the fairy's hair and dress. Draw her fingers, then add some detail to her face and the edges of her wings.

Step 4

Now add the holes on the wings, and draw the belt, headband, bracelets, and boots. Define the features of the fairy's face.

Step 5

Add further shading to the folds on the fairy's dress and her wings. Add some light shading to her face and her arms and legs.

Step 6

Now you can start to color your fairy. Use a pretty pink for the fairy's dress. Then paint the belt brown, with a red jewel for the buckle. Color the wings light blue and give your fairy golden hair. Use a very light pink for the fairy's skin and a light blue for her pretty eyes.

Step 7

Bring your fairy to life with touches of white to add sparkle. Dot splashes of white around the fairy's wings, hair, and dress. Finish your picture by adding some highlights to the face, arms, legs, wings, and hair. Your pretty water fairy is now complete!

Fun-loving Fairies

Fairies that live in water are also called "sprites" or "nymphs." These fairies can swim underwater like a fish and are full of fun. Some people say they can change their shape to look like an insect or a flower, to help them hide when people are near!

Fire Fairies

Dancing in the flames of any fire are the fire fairies. These spritely little creatures love the crackle, heat, and color of a fire. Fire fairies are full of fun—but watch out! These mischievous fairies love to play naughty tricks on anyone who might be watching them...

Step 1

Draw your fairy in a leaping pose. Draw her body and dress. Then add her arms, hands, legs, feet, and wings. Add the flame.

Step 2

Mark the fairy's eyes and pencil her dress, belt, and hair. Draw the edge of the flame.

Step 5

Now you can shade your fairy. Add shading to her dress, body, face, and hair. Use shading marks to add a pattern to the wings and flame.

Step 6

Bring your fire fairy to life with color. Use a bright orange for the fairy's hair and eyes. Now color the skin light brown, and the dress a deep, dark brown. Use yellow for the lower arms, hands, feet, flame, and the fairy's wings.

Step 7

Add a red outline to the wings, lower arms, hands, feet, and the flame. Use light orange to add more shading and the pattern marks. Finally, add highlights and color the eyeballs and teeth white.

Firework Fun

Fireworks are a fire fairy's favorite! These fairies love to watch fireworks bang and flash. They jump in and out of the colorful sparks and zoom among the lights in the sky. The next time you watch a firework sparkle in the sky, look out for fire fairies nearby!

Beautiful Mermaids

Deep beneath the ocean waves, mermaids swim in watery caves. For hundreds of years, people have believed in mermaids. Sailors from long ago told tales of mermaids calling to them from the waves. Some even say they saw these beautiful creatures sitting on rocks to comb their hair as they sang!

Step 1
Draw the mermaid reaching up toward the ocean surface. Draw her body and long, fanned tail. Then add her head, arms, and hands.

Step 2
Add the mermaid's eyes and hair and the shape of her hands.

Step 3

Now draw the star in the mermaid's hair, then add the curls of her hair, the belly button, and the area where her tail joins her waist. Draw the mermaid's face and fingers, too.

Step 4

Draw the headband, necklace, and bracelets. Add the pattern on the tail and the lines on its tip.

Step 5

Shade the mermaid's hair, body, arms, face, and tail. Add deeper shading to the jewelry.

Step 6

Color the tail with a beautiful blue-green shade. Use a light brown for the skin and a rich yellow for the mermaid's hair and bracelet. Then color her necklace and headband deep red and her eyes bright blue.

Step 7

Now color the mermaid's teeth bright white and add the whites of her eyes. Use light tints to add highlights to her tail, hair, jewelry, and skin. Your watery beauty is ready to swim the seas!

Forever Young

Mermaids never grow old! They stay young and beautiful forever. They are also very strong and can swim through the ocean waters as quickly as a shark!

Powerful Unicorns

You might mistake a unicorn for a horse, but look a little closer and you'll see the amazing horn on this magical creature's head. You'll never see a unicorn by day—these powerful beasts appear only under moonlight.

Step 1

Draw the unicorn's body, neck, and head. Draw the horn on the head. Then add the legs, hooves, and tail.

Step 2

Pencil the mane, tail, nostrils, ears, and the eye. Draw the curving lines of the unicorn's head, chest, neck, and legs. Erase the rough lines from step 1.

22

Step 5

Start to bring your magical creature to life with shading. Use light strokes to begin with, then add some heavier marks for darker areas.

Step 6

This unicorn is a beautiful pink color. Cover the body with a light pink, then add a deeper shade on its belly, legs, and under its neck. Color the mane and tail purple and the horn brown.

Step 7

Finally, add highlights to the unicorn's mane, tail, body, horn, hooves, and eye. Your graceful unicorn is now complete!

A Unicorn's Magic

Long ago, people believed that a unicorn's horn was so powerful it could cure sick people. By touching the horn of a unicorn, a person could be healed. It was even said that the person might then live forever!

Flying Unicorns

Some magical unicorns have a truly incredible power—they can fly. These amazing creatures have huge wings that they use to lift them up into the air so they can soar through the sky.

Step 1

Draw the unicorn's body, neck, and head. Add the horn on its head. Then draw the legs, hooves, and tail. Add the wings.

Step 2

Add the curving lines of the wings, mane, legs, neck, and tail. Pencil the eye and ear. Erase the rough lines from step 1.

Step 3

Draw the feathery lines at the edge of the unicorn's wings. Add detail to the mane and tail. Draw the mouth, jaw, and nostril.

Step 4

Add more detail to the wings and mane. Draw the lines on the horn and the lines on the unicorn's tail, neck, and face.

Step 5

Shade your unicorn's body, neck, legs, face, mane, and tail. Carefully shade the huge wings to show their feathers.

Step 6

Color your unicorn white. Use gold for the mane and tail, cream for the wings, and dark brown for the hooves and horn.

Step 7

Add white highlights to the wings, mane, and tail. Also give the body and face highlights to bring out the detail in your picture. Your wonderful unicorn is ready to fly!

Unicorn King

The most famous winged unicorn is Pegasus. In Greek legends, Pegasus was a great, powerful unicorn that had many adventures. One day, the king of the Greek gods, named Zeus, turned Pegasus into lots of beautiful stars. If you look up into the night sky, you can see the starry shape of the unicorn!

Glossary

adventures exciting journeys or experiences
antennae the "feelers" on top of a creature's head. Antennae help creatures to feel their way around.
crescents long, curved shapes that look a little like half moons
cure to make well again
detail the fine lines on a drawing
erase to remove
fairies magical, flying creatures that can perform spells
features the eyes, eyebrows, nose, and mouth of a face
fireworks something that makes a display of light or noise when lit with a match or a flame
foxglove a brightly colored flower with large petals
highlights the light parts on a picture
hooves the hard parts on an animal's feet
horn a long, hard, pointed part on a creature's head
insect a creature with wings, six legs, and three parts to its body
magical to do with magic
mermaids beautiful creatures with the tail of a fish and the body and head of a woman. Mermaids live in the oceans.
mischievous loves to play tricks
nostril an opening on an animal's head through which it breathes
pose the position a person or creature is in
rustle the sound that an animal or an object may make as it moves against something
sailors people who sail boats or ships
shading the dark markings on a picture
soar to fly easily through the sky
spritely full of life and energy
stalk the stiff stem of a plant
starry having lots of stars
unicorns magical creatures that look like a horse but which have a horn on their heads. Some unicorns have wings and can fly.
winged to have wings

For More Information

Books

Amazon Digital. *How to Draw a Unicorn In Six Easy Steps* (Kindle Edition). Seattle, Washington: Amazon Digital, 2011.

Soloff Levy, Barbara. *How to Draw Princesses and Other Fairy Tale Pictures: Dover How to Draw*. Mineola, NY: Dover Publications, 2005.

Watt, Fiona. *How to Draw Fairies and Mermaids: Usborne Activities*. London, England: Usborne Books, 2005.

Websites

Find out more about fairies and play lots of fun games on Disney's website at:
disney.go.com/fairies

Find out more about mermaids at:
www.thekidswindow.co.uk/News/Mermaids.htm

Read the story of *The Little Mermaid* at:
www.childrenstory.info/childrenstories/thelittlemermaid.html

Find out more about unicorns at:
www.thekidswindow.co.uk/News/Unicorns.htm

Publisher's note to educators and parents: Our editors have carefully reviewed these websites to ensure that they are suitable for students. Many websites change frequently, however, and we cannot guarantee that a site's future contents will continue to meet our high standards of quality and educational value. Be advised that students should be closely supervised whenever they access the Internet.

Index

art stores 5

clothing 6, 7, 8, 9, 10, 11, 12, 13, 14, 15, 16
color 5, 8, 12, 13, 16, 17, 20, 21, 24, 28, 29

drawing details 7, 8, 11, 12, 15, 16, 19, 20, 22, 23, 24, 27, 28

equipment 5
erasing 5, 6, 10, 22, 26

fairies and fireworks 17
fairies and flowers 9, 13
fairy tricks 9, 13, 14
features 6, 7, 8, 9, 10, 11, 12, 14, 15, 16, 17, 18, 19, 20, 21, 22, 23, 26, 27
fire fairies 14–17
forest fairies 6–9

hiding places 9, 13
highlights 5, 9, 13, 17, 21, 25, 29

jewelry 7, 8, 11, 12, 19, 20, 21

mermaids 4, 5, 18–21
mermaids and sailors 18
mermaid songs 18

Pegasus 29
poses 14, 18

shading 8, 9, 12, 16, 17, 20, 24, 28
stories 4, 29

unicorns 4, 5, 22–29
unicorn horns 22, 23, 24, 25, 26, 27, 28
unicorn powers 25, 26

wands 6, 7
water fairies 10–13
wings 6, 7, 8, 9, 10, 11, 12, 13, 14, 15, 16, 17, 26, 27, 28, 29